TAPPING
THE
WISDOM
OF
GOD

BILL WINSTON

Tapping The Wisdom of God
Bill Winston
ISBN 978-1-5954449-3-6
Copyright © 2013, 2014, 2017, 2018

Bill Winston Ministries
P.O. Box 947
Oak Park, IL 60303-0947

Table of Contents

Introduction

Today we need leaders with real solutions to society's problems. One man said we are coming into a time in history that the problems we have in society are not going to be solved on the same level they were created. In other words, it's going to take "Level Two" solutions to solve "Level One" problems.

God is assigning believers to positions of leadership in business, ministry, education and all spheres of influence, and it's time for believers to manifest the wisdom of God. We should be the problem solvers. We were not created to run from problems, but we run to them because we have access to the answer to every problem in the world. How? Through the **Wisdom of God.** The Bible tells us that "Wisdom is the principal thing" (Proverbs 4:7).

Every challenge and battle you are faced with today requires godly wisdom to overcome it. There is a wisdom which I call "natural human wisdom" that mostly comes through technological experimentation or "trial and error." But the apostle Paul writes in Ephesians 3:10 that the Body of Christ is going to operate in "the manifold wisdom of God" or on a mental frequency that will be far above human wisdom. This display of wisdom will place the Body of Christ in a position of prominence in the world.

God's wisdom is shown to be true by its results. In other words, the proof of wisdom is results. Jesus changed the world because He used godly wisdom and got results. Every child of God has access to the wisdom of God; it's your birthright. And, it's time for you to enjoy this heritage and get results too.

In *Tapping the Wisdom of God,* you will learn how to access God's wisdom for every situation. If you know how to tap into God's wisdom, you can find answers to every challenge or problem you will ever encounter, whether it's in operating your business or ministry, leading in local, state, or federal government, or in managing your personal life. Remember, the wisdom of God is the Word of God; wherever you have His Word you have His wisdom. While reading this book, I encourage you to take a new approach to problems. Don't worry, complain, or talk about how bad things are; instead, ask God for His wisdom and His Word on the situation, and expect results!

Chapter One

Wisdom Always Brings Results

There are three things in the Old Testament that many times go together: 1) Wisdom, 2) Knowledge, and 3) Understanding. In Proverbs 2:6, you'll see these three things listed together, "**For the Lord giveth <u>wisdom</u>: out of his mouth** *cometh* **<u>knowledge</u> and <u>understanding</u>.**"

I'll use this analogy to help you understand how these three things work together:

- **Knowledge** is the parts.
- **Understanding** is the assembling of those parts.
- **Wisdom** is the product or the result of those assembled parts.

For example, you may have a car that you take apart and put back together again, but once it is assembled the car won't start. Well, you still have all the parts of the car (knowledge) but somewhere in the assembly process, something was put back in the wrong place, so now you're unable to get the anticipated results. You have to check your assembly (understanding) and make the correction to get the desired results (wisdom).

If you look at the account of Daniel and the three Hebrew boys, Shadrach, Meshach, and Abednego, who were taken into captivity by King Nebuchadnezzar, you'll see they were chosen for their wisdom, understanding and knowledge. Daniel 1:4 says they were "… **well favoured, and skilful in all wisdom, and cunning in knowledge, and understanding science,…**" But even though they were in captivity, it didn't break their identity with their God. Daniel 1:17 says, "**As for these four children, God gave them knowledge and skill in all learning and wisdom: and Daniel had understanding in all visions and dreams.**" Verse 20 goes on to say, "**And in all matters** of wisdom *and* understanding, that the king enquired of them, he found them ten times better than all the magicians *and* astrologers that *were* in all his realm."

Notice God gave them "knowledge and skill in all learning and wisdom." In all learning— so they had to learn. So <u>you have to learn</u> as well. But God gave them the knowledge and wisdom with their learning. So they could read the same thing that the people who didn't know God could read but be ten times better in understanding than anybody in the king's realm.

So even while you're in school and learning, the spirit of wisdom is on you to get more understanding and more revelation than someone else going to the same school, or in the same class.

<u>Wisdom Is The Principal Thing</u>

In the book of Proverbs, chapter 4, it says, "Get wisdom, get understanding: forget *it* not; neither decline from the words of my mouth. Forsake her not, and she shall preserve thee: love her, and she shall keep thee. Wisdom is the principal thing; *therefore* get wisdom: and with all thy getting get understanding" (verses 5-7).

In verse 7, it says, "Wisdom is the principal thing, therefore get wisdom." When the wisdom of God speaks, it speaks the Word of God, as found in Luke 11:49, because the wisdom of God is the Word. So if we substitute "Word of God" in Proverbs 4:5-7, then the scripture would read something like this: "… Get the Word of God…The Word of God is the principal thing; therefore get the Word of God."

"Principal" means *chief, most important, or considerable.* So the "principal" of something is the most important part. For example, if someone borrows money from a bank, there is principal and there is interest. The principal is the most important part. Without it there is no interest. Or, if you're baking a cake, the flour is the "principal" thing. It's the most important ingredient in the cake, and without it you don't have a cake.

The problem should never become the principal thing or controlling factor. The Word of God should be the controlling factor in every area of our lives. It will control or solve any problem or situation. "Get wisdom, forget it not…wisdom (the Word of God) is the principal thing."

It's the controlling factor given to the believer by God Himself to guarantee your success and victory every time.

If you have a problem, or an impossible situation, don't worry and talk about how bad things are, pray that you will increase in wisdom. For every problem that exists, wisdom has the answer. "Get wisdom, wisdom is the principal thing."

People often try to get wealth without wisdom, and wisdom really should come before anything else. In the book of Proverbs, it speaks about wisdom saying, **"By me kings reign, and princes [rulers] decree justice…I love them that love me; and those that seek me early shall find me. Riches and honour *are* with me…"** (Proverbs 8:15-18). Do you need to know what to do? God's wisdom gives you that and more. It's the ability to use knowledge.

Godly Wisdom Equals Results

Jesus was criticized for associating with sinners, but He used godly wisdom and got results.

> **The Son of man came eating and drinking, and they say, Behold a man gluttonous, and a winebibber, a friend of publicans and sinners. But wisdom is justified of her children.** (Matthew 11:19)

The proof of wisdom is results.

What does the phrase "wisdom is justified of her children" mean? The *Good News Translation* (GNT) reads, **"God's wisdom, however, is shown to be true by its results."** In other words, the proof of wisdom is results. Jesus answered His critics, [my paraphrase], "You tell me that

I'm hobnobbing with sinners, but do you see results?" They saw results!

Remember what Paul said in 1 Corinthians 2:4-5? **"And my speech and my preaching was not with enticing words of man's wisdom, but in demonstration of the Spirit and of power: That your faith should not stand in the wisdom of men, but in the power of God."** In other words, Paul was no longer going to use the wisdom of men in ministering to the people, not when he was a partaker of God's wisdom. Every child of God possesses the wisdom of God, it's your birthright, and it's time the Church begins to enjoy this heritage.

Paul went on to say, **"Howbeit we speak wisdom among them that are perfect: yet not the wisdom of this world, nor of the princes of this world, that come to nought"** (verse 6). This means that man's wisdom doesn't bring the most effective or desired results. We need to operate in God's wisdom whose frequency is on another level, giving results no natural wisdom can give.

For example, when a city attempts to correct its revenue shortfall, man's wisdom says, "build two casinos." Well, this isn't God's wisdom. With this solution, money might be taken from people who can least afford to lose it. Notice, the overall effect is that things get worse. Why? Political and civic leaders are not using the wisdom of God.

To truly fix any broken government, business, or educational system, it takes the wisdom of God. Looking back in history, Egypt was a world leader in scientific and intellectual knowledge. They invented broadcloth, calculus and even embalming fluid. However, no matter how much of man's wisdom they acquired, it was not enough to deliver them from the coming "dearth" or famine recorded in the book of Genesis, chapter 41.

Natural wisdom is not enough to deliver the United States from economic decline. So, who do our leaders call when there aren't sufficient intellectual abilities or enough technological solutions to keep situations from getting worse? At these times, our government and business leaders should be calling the Church, with its arsenal of believers who have proven track records of successfully addressing society's challenges and problems in education, business, government, the sciences and more.

So, what am I saying? The wisdom of God is what the Body of Christ must put to work. We are already partakers. The Bible tells us that Jesus is the wisdom and power of God (1 Corinthians 1:24). Let me share a personal example with you.

I was just starting the Joseph Center and I had a desire to teach black male high-school students about business. It just so happened that about the same time a Chairman and CEO from a Fortune 500 company in the north suburbs had recently attended a private session with key leaders in Chicago during which he was asked, "What are you doing to help the black male youth in your city?" He replied, "Nothing." But his answer bothered him and stayed with him so much, that he told his daughter about the encounter and she asked him the same question.

Later he asked his assistant (one of our church members) what kind of solution she could suggest. She told him, "I don't know, but maybe my pastor knows."

She arranged a meeting between me and the chairman. He began our meeting stating which religious affiliation he was associated with. Then he went on to say, "Reverend, it might be when I get to heaven, Saint Peter might be standing at the gate, and ask me what I did to help these people. I won't have an answer for him, and I need an answer."

It's interesting how God can put something on someone's heart. (I'm telling you, we believers are anointed with the spirit of wisdom to be problem solvers).

I said to him, "I don't know what I can do right now, but give me one week, and I'll know." What was I doing? I was following Daniel's example in the book of Daniel, chapter 2, when the king dreamed a dream that bothered him to such an extent, he was willing to cut the heads off all his wise men, soothsayers and witches because they didn't have an answer for him. In that case, Daniel asked for a night to get the answer. He didn't know what the answer was, but he knew how to get it by faith.

In Proverbs 2:6-7 it reads:

> For the Lord giveth wisdom: out of his mouth *cometh* knowledge and understanding. He layeth up sound wisdom <u>for</u> the righteous: *he is* a buckler to them that walk uprightly.

In James 1:5 it says, "If any of you lack wisdom, let him ask of God..."

See the Lord lays up sound wisdom (that's reserved) for us and all we need to do is "ask." Notice, I asked for wisdom and expected an answer that week. Why?

Because wisdom is part of my inheritance. Then I waited for wisdom's download. The next thing I knew I had a four-page PowerPoint presentation for the chairman.

By the time I got to the fourth page, the chairman said, "I've got $40,000 in the

Chairman's Fund now. Can you take that?" So I set up a bank account to begin a program for the youth. Wisdom! Notice, I didn't have to beg for money. Why? Because with wisdom comes "...riches and honour" (Proverbs 3:16).

The Spirit of Wisdom is Upon Us

It's time for the Church to take the lead. The world is waiting for the "manifestation of the sons of God." The world is not going to have the answers to today's seemingly insurmountable problems. When Jesus came He had answers. He functioned in the power and wisdom of God. Matthew 13:54 reads, **"And when he was come into his own country, he taught them in their synagogue, insomuch that they were astonished, and said, Whence hath this *man* this wisdom, and *these* mighty works?"**

Remember what Jesus said when He opened the book and read from it in the synagogue?

The Spirit of the Lord is upon me, because he hath anointed me to preach the gospel to the poor; he hath sent me to heal the brokenhearted, to preach deliverance to

WISDOM ALWAYS BRINGS RESULTS | 19

the captives, and recovering of sight to the blind, to set at liberty them that are bruised, To preach the acceptable year of the Lord. (Luke 4:18-19)

The anointing that was on Jesus is the same anointing that came upon you and me when we received salvation and were baptized in the Holy Ghost. Isaiah, chapter 10, reads, **"And it shall come to pass in *that* day, that his burden shall be taken away from off thy shoulder, and his yoke from off thy neck, and the yoke shall be destroyed because of the anointing"** (verse 27). The anointing is the burden-removing, yoke-destroying power of God. Isaiah 11:1-2 goes on to say, **"And there shall come forth a rod out of the stem of Jesse, and a Branch shall grow out of his roots"** (Isaiah 11:1). Jesse was King David's father. Jesus is often called "the Son of David." The branch is the Church (i.e. the Body of Christ). **"And the <u>spirit of the Lord</u> shall rest upon him, <u>the spirit of wisdom</u> and <u>understanding</u>, <u>the spirit of counsel</u> [<u>needed when you confront a legal issue</u>] and <u>might</u> [<u>that's the ability to</u>**

do anything], **the spirit of knowledge** and **of the fear of the Lord** [that keeps you on track]" (Isaiah 11:2). All of these anointings were on Jesus, but now the anointing has come on His Body (the Church, or the believers).

God's anointing does several things:

- **It gives** you an ability that will bring you to prominence,
- **It enables** you to become mentally productive like never before,
- **It illuminates** your mind, and
- **It imparts** to you creative abilities and witty inventions.

In short, the anointing is the "performance enhancer." God's anointing and His wisdom gives you the ability to excel wherever you are placed. It doesn't matter where you are. Remember, the proof of God's wisdom is results and every person with results automatically gains respect.

I decree from this day forward, you will have the anointing of wisdom functioning in your life.

In 1 Samuel, chapter 16, Samuel went to Bethlehem to anoint somebody who was to take King Saul's place.

Again, Jesse made seven of his sons to pass before Samuel. And Samuel said unto Jesse, The Lord hath not chosen these. And Samuel said unto Jesse, Are here all *thy* children? And he said, There remaineth yet the youngest, and, behold, he keepeth the sheep. And Samuel said unto Jesse, Send and fetch him: for we will not sit down till he come hither. (verses 10-11)

Now this is interesting because in your life, <u>you too have been chosen</u>. In John 15:16 (*GOD'S WORD Translation*) Jesus says, "You didn't choose me, but I chose you." Chosen means to be picked out of a group. Don't think it is a coincidence that you are positioned where you are in your school, workplace, home or community. It's the divine plan of God. You didn't choose Him, He chose you. Not only that, He's gifted you, and the giftings He gave you are without repentance; they are for life. He sends you into the world and your sphere of influence to transform it. Your gifts are to be used wherever He sends, plants or places you, not just behind the four walls of the church.

1 Samuel 16:12-13 says,

And he sent, and brought him in. Now he was ruddy, *and* withal of a beautiful countenance, and goodly to look to. And the Lord said, Arise, anoint him: for this is he. Then Samuel took the horn of oil, and anointed him in the midst of his brethren: and the Spirit of the Lord came upon David from that day forward. So Samuel rose up, and went to Ramah.

It's kind of interesting that my middle name is Samuel. I think that it's more than a coincidence that I'm here to bring you a word that will cause faith to come and activate the anointing Jesus placed on you as a part of your redemption. The apostle Paul said that in the last days, the manifold wisdom of God is to be manifested through the Church (Ephesians 3:10), revealing a better way of doing whatever job there is to be done.

⊰ Chapter Two ⊱

Wisdom is Your Inheritance

In Luke, chapter 21, it says, **"For I will give you a mouth and wisdom, which all your adversaries shall not be able to gainsay nor resist"** (verse 15). Now do you see why the Pharisees and high priests hated Jesus and wanted to kill Him? He spoke with such wisdom that His critics were unable to snare Jesus in His words. And when you speak with God's wisdom, people will listen to you. One man said, "wisdom will establish your prominence even among your enemies."

Ephesians, chapter 3, reads:

Unto me, who am less than the least of all saints, is this grace given, that I should preach among the Gentiles the unsearchable riches of Christ;

And to make all *men* see what *is* the fellowship of the mystery, which from the beginning of the world hath been hid in God, who created all things by Jesus Christ: To the intent that now unto the principalities and powers in heavenly *places* might be known by the church the manifold [many sided] wisdom of God. (verses 8-10)

Now let's look again at 1 Corinthians, chapter 2. It says:

Howbeit we speak wisdom among them that are perfect: yet not the wisdom of this world, nor of the princes of this world, that come to nought: But we speak the wisdom of God in a mystery, *even* the hidden *wisdom,* which God ordained before the world unto our glory: Which none of the princes of this world knew: for had they known *it,* they would not have crucified the Lord of glory. (verses 6-8)

Notice in the verses I just quoted, satan inspired men to crucify Jesus. Why? The enemy thought he was killing and removing Jesus forever from this earth. However, the wisdom of God had satan playing right into God's hand. The enemy didn't kill Jesus, he planted Him. What seemed like a tragedy was really a triumph. God's plan needed someone to plant Jesus as a sacrificial lamb, but it couldn't be just anybody, it had to be the high priest. In the Old Testament, high priests were responsible for preparing the sacrifice. That's the wisdom of God. Satan couldn't stop Jesus. Satan lost his wisdom when he got thrown out of heaven. The Bible says he was the anointed cherub that covered the throne. But when he rebelled against God, the anointing left and he left heaven. So now he only has his wisdom. But you and I have God's wisdom.

1 Corinthians 2:16 also says, you have the mind of Christ. That's the same mind that created the world. Why? Because wisdom is key for you doing the things that God wants you to do. Confess this now, "I have the mind of Christ."

> **Wisdom is not something that's hidden from you. It's something that's hidden for you.**

Luke 11:49 says, **"Therefore also said the wisdom of God, I will send them prophets and apostles, and** *some* **of them they shall slay and persecute."** This was written in the Scriptures. The wisdom of God is the Word of God imparted by the Holy Ghost.

Wisdom is not something that's hidden from you. It's something that's hidden for you. In Proverbs, chapter 2, it says, **"He layeth up sound wisdom for the righteous: he** *is* **a buckler to them that walk uprightly"** (verse 7). So the wisdom of God is laid up for you right now!

Wisdom is part of your inheritance. It is part of what Jesus died to provide. In Revelation, chapter 5, it says, **"Saying with a loud voice, Worthy is the Lamb that was slain to receive power, and riches, and wisdom, and strength, and honour, and glory, and blessing"** (verse 12).

Jesus was slain (crucified) to redeem

humanity because of the sin of Adam. Everything that mankind lost when Adam fell, Jesus Christ got it back. The wisdom of God is now available to you and is part of your inheritance.

You are made to solve problems, and you, and the God that dwells in you, can solve anything (Genesis 41:15-16). See the problem with a different attitude instead of frustration and worry; appropriate faith and have expectation that God will give you an answer (Daniel 2:16-23).

God is ready to bring you to prominence. He is ready to bring you to leadership and have you solve the problems that the world cannot solve with intellectual knowledge that is limited to secular book knowledge. But you were never designed to walk in book knowledge without godly knowledge. The enemy has cleverly tried to take God out of the educational system, out of the business world, out of politics, government, entertainment, and the family, but we are putting Him back into everything!

Wisdom is one of the things Jesus died to provide for you.

God's wisdom should be applied to everything we do. Without the wisdom of God, you cannot see all aspects of a problem. You operate in gaps when you don't operate in wisdom.

Wisdom will not only tell you what to say, but tell you how to say it. You could forfeit better solutions and answers if you are only using natural wisdom to solve problems and make decisions. This could result in the enemy keeping back part of your inheritance.

Today, we need the wisdom of God on how to raise our children. How many parents are at their wits end as to what to do in raising their teenager, or younger kids for that matter? We are living in a time when the world is drifting further away from the wisdom of God, and we are seeing the results of unwise living with increased poverty, diseases, divorces, broken families, and the creation of ungodly laws.

Jesus said, "As long as I am in the world, I am the light of the world" (John 9:5). He took personal responsibility for the darkness in the earth. He went on to say in another Gospel, "Ye are the light of the world" (Matthew 5:14), speaking to His disciples and us. Christianity was never meant to be dictated but to be demonstrated. The world should look to God's people, who have God's wisdom, for an example and for leadership.

> But as it is written, Eye hath not seen, nor ear heard, neither have entered into the heart of man, the things which God hath prepared for them that love him. But God hath revealed *them* unto us by his Spirit: for the Spirit searcheth all things, yea, the deep things of God. (1 Corinthians 2:9-10)

The Holy Spirit is the One who orchestrates the wisdom of God. "For what man knoweth the things of a man, save the spirit of man which is in him? even so the things of God knoweth no man, but the Spirit of God. Now we have received, not the spirit of the world, but the spirit which is of God; that we might know the things that are freely given to us of God" (1 Corinthians 2:11-12).

Even as a 12-year-old child, Jesus had wisdom that astounded the people in the Temple. Remember, He wasn't functioning as God but as a man. So, a person can be 12 years old and receive and function in the wisdom of God and astound adults. Just because a person is old in age and gray-headed doesn't mean they have wisdom. It's the Holy Spirit that imparts wisdom. "Great men are not *always* wise: neither do the aged understand judgment" (Job 32:9). "But *there is* a spirit in man: and the inspiration of the Almighty giveth them understanding" (Job 32:8).

Another example of someone who accessed the wisdom of God was the Greek (Syrophenician Gentile) woman found in Mark, chapter 7. It says,

> And from thence he arose, and went into the borders of Tyre and Sidon, and entered into an house, and would

have no man know *it:* but he could not be hid.

For a *certain* woman, whose young daughter had an unclean spirit, heard of him, and came and fell at his feet: The woman was a Greek, a Syrophenician by nation; and she besought him that he would cast forth the devil out of her daughter.

But Jesus said unto her, Let the children first be filled: for it is not meet to take the children's bread, and to cast it unto the dogs. (verses 24-27)

However you slice it, this Gentile woman was being called a dog, which was a Jewish expression for the Gentiles of that day. Notice however, this woman did not get offended. When you are offended you cannot operate in real faith, which is needed for anyone to receive God's wisdom. I believe that when a person is walking in the God-kind of faith you cannot offend them.

So the woman replies to Jesus:

...Yes, Lord: yet the dogs under the table eat of the children's crumbs. And he said unto her, For this saying go thy way; the devil is gone out of thy daughter. And when she was come to her house, she found the devil gone out, and her daughter laid upon the bed. (Mark 7:28-30)

Her daughter was healed! What did she access? She accessed a Word that Jesus could not resist. Jesus said, **"<u>For this saying</u> go thy way; the devil is gone out of thy daughter."**

This woman was a Greek, not a Jew, and was outside the covenant. It was not yet her time to receive "the children's bread." Romans 1:16 says the Word of God came to the Jew <u>first</u>, then to the Greek. It was not her time. But by faith, she accessed the wisdom of God and broke through the time barrier to receive her answer. What was the result? Her daughter was delivered.

When was the wisdom of God deposited in the unseen realm for you, me and the

Syrophenician woman? It was deposited before the foundation of the world. How did this mother access God's wisdom? What tool did she use? Faith! Now you can see that **every answer was here before the problem.**

The wisdom of God is available to you to access in any situation at anytime and any place where you are getting resistance. You can go and get the wisdom of God and get your breakthrough. There is a solution to your problem, and you can get the answer right now.

God chose you before the foundation of the world, and you were blessed with all spiritual blessings before the foundation of the world.

Blessed *be* the God and Father of our Lord Jesus Christ, who hath blessed us with all spiritual blessings in heavenly *places* in Christ: According as he hath chosen us in him before the foundation of the world, that we should be holy and without blame before him in love. (Ephesians 1:3-4)

Chapter Three

How to Get Wisdom

God's wisdom is available for any challenge, problem, or task you encounter in your business, ministry or home. But how do we get access to God's wisdom? There are several ways.

Meditate God's Word

In the Old Testament, when God turned over the leadership of the children of Israel to Moses' protégé, Joshua, God instructed Joshua on the key ingredient for his success:

> **This book of the law shall not depart out of thy mouth; but thou shalt meditate therein day and night, that thou mayest observe to do according to all that is written therein: for then thou shall make thy way prosperous,**

and then thou shalt have good success.
(Joshua 1:8)

The *Amplified Bible* says, "**...you shall deal wisely *and* have good success.**"

Meditation of God's Word (biblical meditation) was the key ingredient to Joshua's success and it was something Israel was commanded (not an option) to do while they worked during the day and in the quiet hours of the night.

God commanded it throughout the history of His people.

Abraham meditated on the stars that God showed him, when He said "**...Look now toward heaven, and tell the stars, if thou be able to number them: and he said unto him, So shall thy seed be**" (Genesis 15:5).

Isaac went out to meditate just before dusk. This was probably a custom that was handed down from his father Abraham. "**And Isaac went out to meditate in the field at eventide...**" (Genesis 24:63). Why? Meditation gave them the wisdom of God for every situation.

In the book of Psalms, David writes, "I call to remembrance my song in the night: I commune (meditate) with mine own heart: and my spirit made diligent search" (Psalm 77:6). "Mine eyes prevent the night watches that I might meditate in thy word" (Psalm 119:148).

For David, meditation was a time of fellowship with the Lord, a time of worship and praise, which draws the presence of God. When we meditate, our spirit makes diligent search. This is our heart (spirit) reaching for answers or making new discoveries in God's Word.

David said, "I will meditate on all Your work And muse on [chew on] Your deeds" (Psalm 77:12 NASB). Whenever the Scriptures read, "I will," it means that you have the decision to make. The choice is yours. The Scriptures advise us to always choose the Word of God and believe only what it says.

Biblical meditation is also designed to renew your mind, and expand your capacity to receive. It is a way to transform your thinking, so you can think on a higher level—on the frequency of God. Some years back God showed me a shopping mall, which frankly was too big for my mind to conceive. He then showed me that meditation was the key to my success. He led me to Joshua 1:3 which I began meditating. The next thing I know I saw the mall as ours and was given a strategy **(God's wisdom)** to possess it. **Remember, if something is too big for your mind, it is too big for your hand.**

Ask God In Faith

"If any of you lack wisdom, let him ask of God, that giveth to all *men* liberally, and upbraideth not; and it shall be given him" (James 1:5).

The second way to get wisdom is to ask God. In every situation in the Bible where God's wisdom is used, a supernatural solution was found or a godly decision was made. In 2 Chronicles, chapter 1, Solomon is taking rule over his father David's kingdom. He had some pretty big shoes to fill, but read what he asks God:

In that night did God appear unto Solomon, and said unto him, Ask what I shall give thee. And Solomon said unto God, Thou has shewed great mercy unto David my father, and hast made me to reign in his stead.

Now, O lord God, let thy promise unto David my father be established: for thou hast made me king over a people like the dust of the earth in multitude. Give me now wisdom and knowledge, that I may go out and come in before this people: for who can judge this thy people *that* is so great?

And God said to Solomon, Because this was in thine heart, and thou hast not asked riches, wealth, or honour, nor the life of thine enemies, neither yet hast asked long life; but hast asked wisdom and knowledge for thyself, that thou mayest judge my people, over whom I have made thee king:

Wisdom and knowledge is granted unto thee; and I will give thee riches, and wealth, and honour, such as none of the kings have had that *have been* before thee, neither shall there any after thee have the like. (verses 7-12)

God answers Solomon, saying all the riches, wealth and honor will come to him along with wisdom. **Many people ask for money and wealth, but what they really need is more wisdom and understanding. They need to be connected to God by having an open and active spiritual frequency through which God can speak to them so they will hear and know what to do in any given situation.**

In 1 Kings, chapter 3, it says,

And the speech pleased the Lord, that Solomon had asked this thing. And God said unto him, Because thou hast asked this thing, and hast not asked for thyself long life; neither hast asked riches for thyself, nor hast asked the life of thine enemies; but hast asked for thyself understanding to discern judgment; Behold, I have done according to thy words: lo, I have given thee a wise and an understanding heart.... (verses 10-12)

Solomon's wisdom was legendary.

Then came there two women, *that were* harlots, unto the king, and stood before him. And the one woman said, O my lord, I and this woman dwell in one house; and I was delivered of a child with her in the house.

And it came to pass the third day after that I was delivered, that this woman was delivered also: and we *were* together; *there was* no stranger with us in the house, save two in the house. And this woman's child died in the night; because she overlaid it.

And she arose at midnight, and took my son from beside me, while thine handmaid slept, and laid it in her bosom, and laid her dead child in my bosom.... And the other woman said, Nay; but the living *is* my son, and the dead is thy son.... And the king said, Bring me a sword. And they brought a sword before the king. And the king said, Divide the living child in two, and give half to the one, and half to the other.

Then spake the woman whose the living child *was* unto the king, for her bowels yearned upon her son, and she said, O my Lord, give her the living child, and in no wise slay it. But the other said, Let it be neither mine nor thine, *but* divide *it.* Then the king answered and said, Give her the living child, and in no wise slay it: she is the mother thereof.

And all Israel heard of the judgment which the king had judged; and they feared the king: for they saw that the

wisdom of God *was* **in him, to do judgment.** (verses 16-28)

Notice, Solomon asked for wisdom, in faith, and God answered. Did he feel anything? No. **Solomon acted in faith. And when he placed a demand on the wisdom that he received from God, it flowed.** He supplied the answer to an impossible situation. This takes "conflict resolution" to a new level.

In Daniel, chapter 2, King Nebuchadnezzar dreamed a dream and he forgot what he dreamed, and it bothered him. He knew there was something significant about this dream. So he asked the wise men, magicians, astrologers, soothsayers, and Chaldeans if they could tell him what he dreamed. All of them were unable to tell or interpret the dream. So the world cannot solve certain problems.

Then Daniel answered with counsel and wisdom to Arioch the captain of the king's guard, which was gone forth to slay the wise *men* of Babylon: He answered and said to Arioch the king's

captain, Why is the decree *so* hasty from the king? Then Arioch made the thing known to Daniel.

Then Daniel went in, and desired of the king that he would give him time, and that he would shew the king the interpretation. Then Daniel went to his house, and made the thing known to Hananiah, Mishael, and Azariah, his companions:

That they would desire mercies of the God of heaven concerning this secret; that Daniel and his fellows should not perish with the rest of the wise *men* of Babylon. [Notice, Daniel asked God in faith.]

Then was the secret revealed unto Daniel in a night vision. Then Daniel blessed the God of heaven. (verses 14-19)

Once you ask God in faith, God will give you (just like He gave Daniel) wisdom in a dream (night vision), if necessary. If you can't hear the frequencies while you are awake, He can wait until you're asleep.

Praying In The Spirit

God's wisdom is also available to you by praying in tongues. In 1 Corinthians, chapter 14, it says, **"Follow after charity, and desire spiritual *gifts*, but rather that ye may prophesy. For he that speaketh in an *unknown* tongue speaketh not unto men, but unto God: for no man understandeth *him;* howbeit in the spirit he speaketh mysteries"** (verses 1-2).

What are mysteries? They are hidden truths. When you pray in tongues you speak in mysteries. People don't understand the mysteries of God because these mysteries operate much above the normal intellectual ability of men. **"Wherefore let him that speaketh in an *unknown* tongue pray that he may interpret. For if I pray in an *unknown* tongue, my spirit prayeth, but my understanding is unfruitful"** (verses 13-14).

You can pray in an unknown tongue and converse with God. There is an answer to every problem. Romans, chapter 8, teaches:

Likewise the Spirit also helpeth our infirmities [or weakness of the flesh]: for we know not what we should pray for as we ought: but the Spirit itself maketh intercession for us with groanings which cannot be uttered. And he that searcheth the hearts knoweth what is the mind of the Spirit, because he maketh intercession for the saints according to *the will of* God. And we know that all things work together for good to them that love God, to them who are the called according to *his* purpose. (verses 26-28)

Proverbs 20:5 also speaks to what happens when we pray in tongues,

Counsel in the heart of man *is like* deep water; but a man of understanding will draw it out.

After you pray in the Spirit, listen for God to give you a word. The Holy Ghost knows you and the situation. The Holy Spirit makes intercession for the saints according to the will of God. Always keep in mind, the answer to your problem is always the will of God—when you meditate or ask for His wisdom or pray in tongues, allow God to speak to you, and then open your mouth.

Praying in tongues was the method I used when we were told by the local government officials that we could not hold services in the shopping center we had purchased. Through praying in the Spirit, God told me what to do and say. I did it and a miracle took place. We had no more delays and through wisdom we got the "green light."

Laying On of Hands

There is yet a final way to acquire the wisdom of God, and that is through the "laying on of hands." Deuteronomy 34:9 reads, **"And Joshua the son of Nun was full of the spirit of wisdom; for Moses had laid his hands upon him...."**

A Word About Wisdom and Might

"Daniel answered and said, Blessed be the

name of God for ever and ever: for wisdom and might are his" (Daniel 2:20). Why do you think "might" is mentioned along with wisdom? Might is a kind of anointing, like wisdom. It is one of the seven spirits described in Isaiah 11:2. <u>Wisdom</u> produces the way you do something and <u>might</u> is the power to make it happen. You see, your destiny is not in the hands of the government or the economy, but in your own hands.

Daniel went on to say:

And he changeth the times and the seasons: he removeth kings, and setteth up kings: he giveth wisdom unto the wise, and knowledge to them that know understanding: He revealeth the deep and secret things: he knoweth what is in the darkness, and the light dwelleth with him. I thank thee, and praise thee, O thou God of my fathers, who hast given me wisdom and might, and hast made known unto me now what we desired of thee: for thou hast *now* made

known unto us the king's matter.
(verses 21-23)

So Daniel received honor. The king promoted Daniel, making him ruler over the whole province of Babylon, and chief of the governors and over all the wise men and soothsayers of Babylon (Daniel 2:46-49). At one time they tried to kill him and he was put in the lion's den. Did he die? No. He had length of days by operating in wisdom.

Wherever God has placed you, you are sent to break the curse off that place. Or whatever assignment He has given you, the wisdom of God and might are what you will need to move forward. Don't rely on flesh, or the wisdom of men. Rely on the voice of God and His wisdom.

In summary, you access God's wisdom by:

- **Meditating God's Word.**
  Joshua 1:8; Psalm 119:148; Psalm 77:6, 12

- **Asking God in Faith.**
  James 1:5-7; 2 Chronicles 1:7-12; 1 Kings 3

- **Praying in the Spirit** (Tongues).
  Romans 8:26-28

- **Laying on of Hands.**
  Deuteronomy 34:9

⊰ Chapter Four ⊱

Wisdom Brings Honor
and Favor

Can you see how our God has given us unlimited access to His wisdom, to provide solutions and direction to any situation on earth?

In the book of Genesis, chapter 41, we read where Pharaoh had a dream and he didn't know what he dreamed or what it meant. He was told about a man in prison (Joseph) who could interpret dreams:

> **Then Pharaoh sent and called Joseph, and they brought him hastily out of the dungeon: and he shaved *himself,* and changed his raiment, and came in unto Pharaoh. And Pharaoh said unto Joseph, I have dreamed a dream, and there is none that can interpret it: and I have heard say of thee, *that* thou canst**

understand a dream to interpret it. (verses 14-15)

So, what happened? Joseph told him the dream and the interpretation.

And the thing was good in the eyes of Pharaoh, and in the eyes of all his servants. And Pharaoh said unto his servants, Can we *find such a one* as this *is,* a man in whom the Spirit of God is? And Pharaoh said unto Joseph, Forasmuch as God hath shewed thee all this, *there is* none so discreet and wise as thou *art:*

Thou shalt be over my house, and according unto thy word shall all my people be ruled: only in the throne will I be greater than thou. And Pharaoh said unto Joseph, See, I have set thee over all the land of Egypt.

And Pharaoh took off his ring from his hand, and put it upon Joseph's hand, and arrayed him in vestures of fine

linen, and put a gold chain about his neck. (verses 37-42)

The story of Joseph also illustrates that God's wisdom brings you to honor (Proverbs 8:18).

The story of Queen Esther is another example of when the wisdom of God brought honor. Queen Esther was used by God to save her people, a woman "chosen for such a time as this." When alerted about Haman's plan to kill the Jews in her kingdom, Esther went against royal protocol and entered into the king's court unannounced.

The king (because of God's favor) pointed his scepter at her and allowed her to enter. With wisdom, Esther invited the king to a banquet (Esther 5:2, 4). She didn't enter his presence "bad-mouthing" Haman. No, that would not have been godly wisdom. Instead, wisdom said, "Please come to dinner."

In 1 Kings, chapter 10, the Queen of Sheba came to visit Solomon, with a very great train of spices, an hundred and twenty talents of gold, and precious stones. **"…she communed with him of all that was in her heart. And**

Solomon told her all her questions: there was not *any* thing hid from the king, which he told her not" (verses 2-3). What was the Queen doing? She was coming to Solomon with her government's problems. And he was giving her the answers. Wow, that's what our government needs: wisdom.

Favor will cause people to change policies and rules on your behalf without regard for their own welfare. I remember needing the wisdom of God in the purchase of our shopping mall and the home of our worship center. The church had just signed the deal and paid our money when without warning we were told by the local village officals that we would not be able to hold services in the new facility. The City Council had voted that our church could not hold worship services in the mall, and a police order was issued to prevent us from moving in.

I prayed in the Holy Ghost for God's wisdom to reveal a solution. The Holy Spirit told me how to respond (what to write and what to say). I called a meeting with the mayor and when I met with her and read the scripture the Holy Spirit had given me, God's favor moved her to make a decision counter to the City Council's vote. We held our first church service in our new building on New Year's Eve night.

The life of Jesus also illustrates that wisdom and favor go together. Luke 2:52, says, **"And Jesus increased in wisdom and stature, and in favour with God and man."** As I said in an earlier chapter, even as a 12-year-old boy, Jesus' wisdom astounded the Temple teachers and priests.

Why couldn't the priests get Jesus' wisdom? They could have, if they had not tried to build their own kingdom. **When you are trying to build your own kingdom, you negate the wisdom of God.** One cannot get the wisdom of God operating in selfishness and wrong motives; the wisdom of God works by love.

A second reason is because they had pride. They had the Torah[1] (knowledge). They were life-long, dedicated students and teachers

---

[1] Torah defined as the five books of Moses; collective body of Jewish teachings in the Hebrews Bible for direction, teaching, instruction and doctrine. (www.torahresourcesinternational.info/definition.

of the book for understanding. But they couldn't put those parts (i.e., knowledge and understanding) together and get wisdom. **Pride in your education, your ability or your intelligence negates the wisdom of God.** To receive God's wisdom you have to become like a child, willing to listen and be taught.

The final reason that the priests could not access the wisdom of God was that they were not seeking it. They didn't desire it. One man said, what you do not desire you do not deserve. Proverbs 18:1 says: **"Through desire a man, having separated himself, seeketh *and* intermeddleth with all wisdom."** The religious leaders thought they knew it all. Remember, the priests were living a little better, but they were sinners like everyone else. And their pride and arrogance blocked the wisdom of God.

Embrace Wisdom

Two famous men that didn't allow their intelligence, education or ability to block God's wisdom were Tuskegee University founder, Booker T. Washington and Tuskegee professor

Dr. George Washington Carver. Their lives demonstrated how honor and favor were bestowed upon these humble men because they were willing to let God's wisdom guide them.

In 1885, Booker T. Washington (a man born in slavery) founded a school for blacks and ex-slaves that not only offered the traditional academic courses, but also required students to learn industry and trade skills. In addition, daily morning devotionals and evening prayers were also required. By requiring each student to master at least two trades, Washington ensured they would always be able to contribute to the betterment of society and be self-supporting after graduation. Booker T. Washington tied "book learning" with the wisdom of God.[2] The results were that in 1905 Tuskegee University turned out more "self-made" millionaires than Yale, Harvard, and Princeton combined. By 1915, twenty years after starting this school, Washington had built 107 buildings (with bricks made by his students), on 2,000 acres of land, with an

2 Rick Williams, with Jared C. Crooks; *Christian Business Legends* (Ashland, Ohio, Business Reform and The Business Reform Foundation; 2004).

enrollment of 1,500 students along with 200 teachers and professors.[3]

Dr. George Washington Carver, was an agriculture chemist who revolutionized the economy of the South by introducing hundreds of uses for the peanut, soybean, pecan, and sweet potato in the place of cotton. These crops replenished the soil and provided income for the South that grew to hundreds of millions of dollars. Dr. Carver's discoveries from the peanut (over 300), the sweet potato (over 118), as well as from the soybean...included things like face powder, instant coffee, and non-toxic colors from which crayons were eventually developed.[4]

In 1921, Dr. Carver accepted an invitation to address the United States Ways and Means Committee in Washington D.C. on the potential uses of the peanut and other crops. Initially he was given 20 minutes to talk, but after hearing what he had to say, the chairman said "go ahead brother, your time is unlimited." Dr. Carver spoke for an hour and forty-five minutes. The

───────────

3 Ibid.

4 William J. Federer, *George Washington Carver: His Life & Faith in His Own Words* (St. Louis, MO: Amerisearch, Inc., 2008), pages 9,18-19.

Chairman of the committee asked him, "How did you learn all these things?" "From an old book," he answered. "What book?" a Senator asked. Carver replied, "The Bible." The Senator then asked, "Does the Bible teach us about peanuts?" "No sir, but it tells us about the God who made the peanut. I asked Him to show me what to do with the peanut and He did."[5]

Dr. Carver was visited at Tuskegee by President Franklin D. Roosevelt and Vice President Calvin Coolidge. He became a confidante and advisor to leaders and scientists from all over the world including Henry Ford and Thomas Edison.[6]

So both Dr. Carver and Booker T. Washington asked for and received wisdom and divine guidance. Proverbs 4:7-8 AMP teaches us, **"For skillful and godly Wisdom is the principal thing...exalt her, and she will exalt and promote you; she will bring you to honor when you embrace her."**

5 Ibid., page 44

6 William J. Federer, *America's God and Country: Encyclopedia of Quotations* rev. ed (Coppell, TX: FAME Publishing, Inc., 1994; St. Louis, MO: Amerisearch, Inc., 2000), page 94. Citations refer to the Amerisearch edition.

Tapping Into God's Frequency

In Proverbs 3:13-14 it says:

Happy *is* the man *that* findeth wisdom, and the man *that* getteth understanding. For the merchandise of it is better than the merchandise of silver, and the gain thereof than gold.

So, wisdom is better than gold, and wisdom is better than money.

She *is* more precious than rubies: and all the things thou canst desire are not to be compared unto her. Length of days is in her right hand; *and* in her left hand riches and honour. Her ways *are* ways of pleasantness, and all her paths *are* peace. (verses 15-17)

The wisdom of man is what we often try to rely on; however, God's wisdom is the frequency we must tap into. Ask yourself, "Is my frequency open to the frequency of God's wisdom?" Whatever your situation, you can ask the Holy Spirit in faith to search in the supernatural realm for an answer to your problem, like you would search for a library book.

God is Jehovah Jireh. He had the solution to your problem before it even existed. He's the God who sees and provides just as He did for Daniel. When he needed God's wisdom, God revealed the answer to him in a night vision.

Conclusion

So keep seeking the wisdom of God. He is about to raise you up. God has made you so that the anointing of God is on your life for everything.

When you don't know what to do, go to God, and place a demand on the wisdom of God. According to Mark 11:24, "...What things soever ye desire, when ye pray, believe that ye receive *them,* and ye shall have *them.*"

Each morning confess that you have the wisdom of God. A scripture I say almost daily is Ephesians 1:17-19:

> That the God of our Lord Jesus Christ, the Father of glory, may give unto you the spirit of wisdom and revelation in the knowledge of him: The eyes of your understanding being enlightened; that ye may know what is the hope of

his calling, and what the riches of the glory of his inheritance in the saints, And what *is* the exceeding greatness of his power to us-ward who believe....

So, believe that you receive wisdom. Pray in the Spirit and listen for God. Then thank God for His mercy and blessing! My prayer for you is that you tap, right now, into the wisdom of God for any situation troubling you. Ask the Lord to release His wisdom into your life so that you will know the way out. Expect Him to give you an answer, speedily.

In closing, remember that God always expects us to give Him the credit. Don't allow pride or fear to keep you from honoring God. There is no limit to what God will do for you, if you'll give Him the glory.

Proverbs 3:13-19

Happy *is* the man *that* findeth wisdom, and the man *that* getteth understanding.

You will get happiness and joy because you have found wisdom.

For the merchandise of it is better than the merchandise of silver, and the gain thereof than fine gold.

Sometimes people seek money. Seek first the kingdom of God, and there you will find the money after discovering the wisdom of God.

She is more precious than rubies: and all the things thou canst desire are not to be compared unto her.

Length of days is in her right hand; *and* in her left hand riches and honour.

Not only will wisdom bring you riches, it will give you honor.

Her ways *are* ways of pleasantness, and all her paths *are* peace.

You can tell when you hit wisdom because there will be a peace inside.

She is a tree of life to them that lay hold upon her: and happy *is every one* that retaineth her.

The Lord by wisdom hath founded the earth; by understanding hath he established the heavens.

So if you want to fix things in this earth, you need wisdom. The same wisdom that created it, you need that wisdom to fix it.

Prayer of Salvation

If you're reading this and you don't know God, I invite you to pray in faith this prayer of salvation.

Heavenly Father, I come to You in the Name of Your Son, Jesus Christ. You said in Your Word that whosoever shall call upon the Name of the Lord shall be saved (Romans 10:13). I am calling on Jesus right now.

I believe that Jesus died on the cross for my sins, that He was raised from the dead on the third day.

Lord Jesus, I am asking You now, come into my heart. Take control of my life and help me be what You want me to be. I repent of my sins and surrender myself totally and completely to You.

I accept You and confess You as my Lord and Savior. Thank You for making me a new person and forgiving me of my sins. In Jesus' Name, Amen.

(Remember to get water baptized as soon as possible according to Acts 16:33.)

Prayer for Baptism of the Holy Spirit

My Heavenly Father, I am Your child, for I believe in my heart that Jesus has been raised from the dead and I have confessed Him as my Lord. Jesus said, "How much more shall your heavenly Father give the Holy Spirit to those who ask Him." I ask You now in the Name of Jesus to fill me with the Holy Spirit.

I step into the fullness and power that I desire in the Name of Jesus. I confess that I am a Spirit-filled Christian. As I yield my vocal organs, I expect to speak in tongues as the Spirit gives me utterance in the Name of Jesus. Praise the Lord! Amen.

Scripture References:

John 14:16-17

Acts 19:2, 5-6

Luke 11:13

1 Corinthians 14:2-15

Acts 1:8

1 Corinthians 14:18,27

Acts 2:4

Ephesians 6:18

Acts 2:32-33, 39

Jude 1:20

Acts 8:12-17

Acts 10:44-46

William (Bill) Samuel Winston

Bill Winston is the visionary founder and senior pastor of **Living Word Christian Center** in Forest Park, Illinois.

He is also founder and president of **Bill Winston Ministries**, a partnership-based global outreach ministry that shares the gospel through television, radio, and the internet; the nationally accredited **Joseph Business School** which has partnership locations on five continents and an online program; the **Living Word School of Ministry** and **Missions; and Faith Ministries Alliance (FMA)**, an organization of more than 800 churches and ministries under his spiritual covering in the United States and other countries.

The ministry owns and operates two shopping malls, **Forest Park Plaza** in Forest Park and **Washington Plaza** in Tuskegee, Alabama. Bill Winston is also the founder and CEO of **Golden Eagle Aviation,** a fixed base operator (FBO) located at the historic Moton Field in Tuskegee.

Bill is married to Veronica and is the father of three, Melody, Allegra, and David, and the grandfather of eight.

Books by Bill Winston

- Born Again and Spirit Filled (Available in English, Polish and Spanish versions)

- Climbing Without Compromise

- Divine Favor – A Gift from God, Expanded Edition

- Faith & The Marketplace

- Imitate God and Get Results (Available in English and French versions)

- Possessing Your Mountain

- Power of the Tongue

- Seeding For the Billion Flow

- Supernatural Wealth Transfer: Restoring the Earth to Its Rightful Owners

- Tapping the Wisdom of God

- The God Kind of Faith, Expanded Edition

- The Kingdom of God In You: Discover the Greatness of God's Power Within

- The Law of Confession: Revolutionize Your Life and Rewrite Your Future with the Power of Words

- The Missing Link of Meditation

- The Power of Grace

- The Power of the Tithe

- The Spirit of Leadership: Leadership Lessons Learned from the Life of Joseph

- Training For Reigning: Releasing the Power of Your Potential

- Transform Your Thinking, Transform Your Life: Radically Change Your Thoughts, Your World, and Your Destiny

Connect With Us!

Connect with Bill Winston Ministries on Social Media. Visit www.billwinston.org/social to connect with all of our official Social Media channels.

Bill Winston Ministries
P.O. Box 947
Oak Park, Illinois 60303-0947
(708) 697-5100
(800) 711-9327
www.billwinston.org

Bill Winston Ministries Africa
22 Salisbury Road
Morningside, Durban, KWA Zulu Natal 4001
+27(0)313032541 orders@bwm.org.za
www.bwm.org.za

Bill Winston Ministries Canada
P.O. Box 2900
Vancouver, BC V6B 0L4
(844) 298-2900
www.billwinston.ca

Prayer Call Center
(877) 543-9443